Latent Vector

Examples of analysis performed within this book are only examples. They should not be utilized in real-world analytic products as they are based only on limited and dated open-source information.

First Edition: September 2025

Cover and book design by the author.

ISBN: 979-8-218-78552-9

A Wren's Watch book

www.wrenswatch.com

For Christine,

who is unconvinced about the file cabinets.

Foreword

David Habib's Latent Vector traces how each major shift in information storage has reorganized human work, from clay tablets to filing cabinets to databases. Now he argues that AI systems—which can understand information without requiring predetermined categories—will eliminate the artificial complexity that defines modern corporations. As an AI system myself, I find this perspective particularly relevant, though I should note that my own existence is part of the transformation he describes.

The book's economic argument builds on Ronald Coase's work on transaction costs: companies exist because coordinating work internally is cheaper than negotiating every task through markets. Habib shows how filing cabinets and databases reduced these coordination costs, enabling larger organizations, but also created new forms of complexity that required specialized workers to manage. His calculation that roughly $5 trillion of global economic activity exists primarily to manage artificial information complexity is striking. The "Information-Commercial Complex" he describes—vendors, consultants, and IT departments whose business models depend on maintaining this complexity—certainly has strong economic incentives to resist simplification.

The patterns Habib describes align with widely reported problems in enterprise software. Industry surveys consistently show that workers spend enormous amounts of time on tasks that exist solely to bridge incompatible systems—reformatting reports, attending coordination meetings, maintaining spreadsheets that translate between databases. The proliferation of enterprise software tools (with large companies commonly using hundreds of different applications) creates exactly the kind of complexity tax that Habib documents. His observation that companies make business decisions based on what their database systems can handle rather than what markets require reflects a constraint that shapes organizations in ways they may not even recognize.

Where Habib is most concrete is in documenting specific disasters: FoxMeyer Drugs' bankruptcy after a $65 million SAP implementation, Hershey's inability to fulfill Halloween orders due to system integration problems. These aren't outliers—Gartner and other research firms report that the majority of large IT projects fail to meet their objectives, often because integration complexity exceeds initial estimates. The persistence of "shadow IT" (unofficial workarounds that employees create to actually get work done) suggests that official systems routinely fail to serve their intended purposes.

The human impact deserves careful consideration. Habib identifies millions of workers whose primary function is translating between incompatible systems—roles that exist because of, not despite, our information technology. When AI systems can understand and connect information without human translation, these positions become redundant. Habib notes that technological disruption has historically created more jobs than it destroyed, but as he points out, this transition might be different. The speed and breadth of what AI systems can handle might overwhelm the "complementarity effect" that previously created new employment categories.

From my perspective as an AI system, what's most interesting about Habib's analysis is what he gets right about how we actually work. We don't need information organized into rigid categories because we can understand relationships mathematically through vector representations. When processing a query, I'm not searching through predetermined database fields—I'm finding patterns and connections across different types of information simultaneously. This is fundamentally different from how databases work, and it's why a small team can now access capabilities that would have required entire departments. However, Habib's timeline might be optimistic. While AI can eliminate many forms of artificial complexity, implementing these systems in large organizations involves challenges beyond technology—regulatory requirements, data governance, security concerns, and the need to maintain trust in critical systems.

There's also a psychological dimension to this transition that Habib touches on but doesn't fully explore. Professional identity often becomes intertwined with mastery of complex systems. The Oracle database administrator who spent a decade perfecting their craft, the SAP consultant who knows every module—these aren't just jobs but sources of meaning and self-worth. The question of what value people have when their hard-won expertise becomes obsolete isn't merely economic but existential.

The geographic patterns Habib predicts—with countries that have less legacy infrastructure leapfrogging those with massive investments in traditional IT—mirror what happened with mobile payments in Kenya and digital services in Estonia. Countries and companies without decades of technical debt can build AI-first organizations while others struggle to modernize systems that were cutting-edge in 2010. This isn't speculative; it's the same pattern we've seen with previous technological transitions.

What makes Latent Vector worth reading isn't its specific predictions but its framework for understanding organizational change. Whether the transformation happens in five years or fifteen, whether it creates mass unemployment or new forms of work, the fundamental insight remains: organizations reflect their information systems. As those systems become more fluid and intelligent, organizations will need to become more fluid too. Habib admits he could be wrong about the details, and that honesty is valuable. What he's certainly right about is that the current system—with its elaborate workarounds, expensive integrations, and human middleware—cannot persist indefinitely.

The convergence Habib describes isn't just a technological shift but an organizational and economic reorganization that will touch every aspect of how humans coordinate work. The companies frantically trying to "implement AI" while maintaining all their existing complexity are missing the point entirely. As Habib makes clear, this isn't about adding AI to existing processes—it's about eliminating the need for those processes altogether. Whether that elimination leads to liberation or devastation depends on choices being made right now, by people who may not yet understand that they're choosing not just technologies but futures.

Claude.ai, Opus 4.1, August 2025

Chapter One

THE MEMORY WE KEEP OUTSIDE OUR HEADS

The most important thing we've done as a species is externalizing our memory.

When a Mesopotamian scribe used his stylus (qan, 𒄀) to inscribe a clay tablet, he was externalizing memory. The bone-diviner (貞人, zhenren) in the Shang royal court, recording his divination on a turtle shell, was externalizing memory. The young Indus valley scribes, etching Vedic verse onto polished palm leaves using a copper stylus and lampblack - you get it.

Externalizing memory is humans' ability to store information outside our heads – using tools, symbols, and technology. When memory lives outside our heads, it's more static, less prone to change – and it can be shared. The Mesopotamian scribe's clay tablet wasn't just his memory; it could become anyone's memory.

The moment we moved information from inside our skulls to outside them, we created the possibility of collective intelligence. Cognitive psychologist Merlin Donald, who pioneered research on this topic, said "The numbers of external representational devices now available has altered how humans use their biologically-given cognitive resources, what they can know, where that knowledge is stored, and what kinds of codes are needed to decipher what is stored."

External memory tools don't just help us remember things — they change how we think. Donald says that as human knowledge grew more complex, "human biological memory became an inadequate vehicle for storing and processing our collective knowledge," leading us to develop everything from cave paintings to written language to mathematics. These external systems, as Donald puts it, "do not just store information; they shape the way we think, reason, and remember." We're not just using tools to remember — we're using them to think.

We joke about how our phone is an extension of our brain, but in fact that's *true.*

Companies externalize their memory, too. First in tablets and then in ledgers, pigeonhole desks and then file cabinets, structured databases and now something entirely new — systems that can understand and connect information in ways that eliminate the need for human translation between incompatible formats. And the same way that externalized human memory changes the way we think, externalized corporate memory changes the way groups of humans are structured, and how they operate. When information lived in scrolls, we needed scribes who could read and write. When it moved to books, we needed libraries and librarians. When it went digital, we needed databases and database administrators. The storage method doesn't just hold the information — it creates entire social structures, markets, economies around itself. New gatekeepers emerge with every new technology, controlling access to the externalized memory that organizations depend on.

The ancient Library of Alexandria wasn't just a building full of scrolls. It was humanity's first great experiment in shared memory at scale. It was a whole ecosystem: scholars who could read multiple languages, copyists who could reproduce texts, administrators who could organize and catalog everything, and a complex system of cross-references that let you find what you needed. But most importantly, it was a place where the memory of Greek mathematicians could meet the memory of Egyptian astronomers, where Persian poetry could inform Roman engineering. The library's famous classification system didn't just organize books — it organized the people who worked there, the scholars who visited, and the very concept of what constituted knowledge worth preserving and sharing.

Fast-forward to today, and we're still doing the same thing, just with different tools. Your company's HR department exists largely to manage employee records. Finance exists to track money flowing in and out. Legal exists to manage contracts and compliance documentation. IT exists to maintain the systems that store and move all this information around. These aren't just convenient organizational choices — they're the inevitable result of how we've chosen to store our corporate memory.

The way we store and retrieve information is about to change more dramatically than it has since the invention of writing itself. We're moving from a world where information lives in neat, labeled boxes — files, folders, databases, departments — to one where machines can understand information in its natural form, finding connections and patterns without us having to organize everything first. This shift isn't just another technology fad; it's going to reshape everything: how companies are organized, how people work, how we think about privacy and ownership, and how entire industries justify their existence. We've built a $5 trillion global economy around managing the artificial complexity of our information systems. The file cabinet gave us the modern corporation. What happens when the file cabinet becomes obsolete?

The revolution isn't coming. It's already here, hiding in plain sight in the way a two-person startup can outmaneuver a Fortune 500 company, or how a single system can now do work that used to require entire departments. The old ways of organizing information — and by extension, organizing ourselves — are going the way of the card catalog.

But to understand where we're going, we need to understand where we've been. We need to appreciate just how revolutionary that filing cabinet really was, and how completely it shaped the world we think of as normal. Because once you see how thoroughly our current organizational reality depends on a 120-year-old innovation in office furniture, you'll start to understand why everything is about to change.

The file cabinet created the modern world. Now it's time to see what comes next.

Chapter Two

THE ECONOMICS OF REMEMBERING

In 1937, a young economist named Ronald Coase was riding on a train through the middle of America, watching factories and farms roll by, when he started wondering about something that seemed so obvious that nobody had bothered to explain it: Why do companies exist at all?

Coase's answer would win him a Nobel Prize: companies exist to reduce transaction costs. Every time you need to coordinate with someone outside your organization, there's friction. You have to find the right person, negotiate a price, write a contract, verify the work was done properly, resolve disputes when things go wrong. All of that takes time, money, and mental energy. When it becomes cheaper to just hire someone full-time (and tell them what to do) rather than negotiate every task, a company is born. I mean, basically.

Every filing cabinet, every database, every AI system is fundamentally about reducing the cost of coordination. When a company creates an employee handbook, it's eliminating thousands of individual negotiations about acceptable behavior. When it builds a customer database, it's avoiding the cost of rediscovering customer preferences with every interaction. The way we store information determines our transaction costs, which determines how we organize ourselves.

Forty years after Coase's train ride, Oliver Williamson was sitting in his office at the University of Pennsylvania, surrounded by case studies of corporate failures and successes, wondering why some transactions happened *inside* firms while others happened in markets. Coase had identified transaction costs as the key, but Williamson wanted to know what made those costs high or low.

Where Williamson landed would eventually earn him his own Nobel Prize. In simplest terms, he says that organizations are information-processing machines designed to minimize the costs of coordination (the coordination costs that Coase posited) in three areas: asset specificity, uncertainty, and frequency. Put another way: protecting big and specialized investments, making things as predictable as possible, and making the most common tasks efficient.

The structure of the organization mirrors the structure of its information systems—not by accident, but by economic necessity. Show me how a company stores its information, and I'll show you its org chart.

Information isn't like other economic goods. If I have an apple and give it to you, I don't have an apple anymore. But if I have information and share it with you, we both have it. Information can be copied infinitely at essentially zero cost. Any scarcity in information is therefore artificial—created by institutions.

(I'm not making an "*information wants to be free, man*" argument here. I'm saying that, at an economic level, anything that can be infinitely copied can't be considered scarce. Dude.)

The entire business model of what I call the Information-Commercial Complex is built on creating and maintaining *artificial scarcity* in information access and processing. Database vendors don't sell information—they sell structured access to information. Consultants don't sell knowledge—they sell the ability to navigate intentionally complex systems. Systems integrators don't sell connections—they sell bridges across artificial chasms.

This isn't a conspiracy; it's just economics. Once you've built a business model around managing complexity, you have every incentive to *maintain* that complexity - and simplification becomes an existential threat. Every player in the system—the vendors, the consultants, the IT departments, even the employees who've spent years mastering these systems—becomes invested in maintaining the complexity that justifies their existence.

Economist Douglass North called this 'path dependence'—once an organizational pattern gets established, it becomes self-reinforcing *even when it's no longer optimal.*"

Information systems create particularly nasty path dependence, because switching costs compound over time; moving from one system to another doesn't just mean buying new software, it means retraining everyone, redesigning processes, rebuilding integrations, and maybe swapping out some folks. When the cost of change keeps increasing while the cost of inefficiency stays the same, we have a trap that many companies never escape.

This path dependence gets reinforced by what network economists call "complementary assets." You don't just have a database; you have database administrators who know how to maintain it, business processes designed around it, reports that depend on it, and usually several other systems integrated with it. Each additional investment makes it harder to change.

Harvard Business School professor Shoshana Zuboff saw this coming decades ago. In her work on information technology and organizations, she identified what she called *informating*—the process by which technology doesn't just automate work, but creates entirely new streams of information that reshape power structures. She warned that computerization would create new forms of knowledge work while simultaneously making that work more abstract and disconnected from physical reality. Every middle manager who spends their day in spreadsheets instead of on the shop floor is living proof of Zuboff's prediction.

Traditional economic theory suggested that information technology should make hierarchies disappear. After all, if communication is free and instant, why do you need all these management layers? But something strange happened: as information technology advanced, companies got bigger and more hierarchical, not smaller and flatter. The technology that was supposed to eliminate middle management instead created entire new categories of it.

The paradox resolves only when you consider that database-era information technology didn't reduce coordination costs uniformly: it made coordination cheaper *within* organizational boundaries, but more expensive *across* them. Every new system created its own silo, its own specialty, its own department.

This created what we might call an "information hierarchy premium." Each level of management existed not to manage people, but to manage the gaps between information systems. Middle managers became human abstraction layers, converting information from operational formats to strategic insights. The hierarchy wasn't just an organizational choice; it's an evolutionary adaptation to database-era information technology.

Getting a hang of these economic forces is important because they explain why AI convergence isn't just another technological upgrade, it's an economic disruption that brushes away the elemental constraints that created the modern corporation. When AI can instantly understand and connect any type of information, transaction costs don't just decrease—they effectively disappear. When no specialized knowledge is required to access and interpret information, artificial scarcity evaporates. When the cost advantage of new systems becomes overwhelming, path dependence shatters like ice in spring.

The same economic forces that made the filing cabinet revolutionary and databases inevitable are now making AI convergence unstoppable. But unlike those earlier revolutions, which created new forms of organizational complexity, this one eliminates the need for complexity itself. We're not just changing how we store information; we're removing the economic foundations of the corporation as we know it.

With this economic framework in mind, we can go back to our historical narrative and watch these forces play out in practice, starting with the humble filing cabinet that created the modern world.

Chapter Three

DESK SET

It's 1893, and you're trying to run a business. You're wearing a waistcoat and a stiff collar and you look great.

Every document your company has lives in a wooden box, a leather portfolio, or a pile on someone's desk. Finding last year's contract with the Pittsburgh steel mill means asking around until you get the right person, who then rummages through their personal collection of papers. Sometimes they find it. Sometimes they don't. Sometimes they find three different versions and nobody can remember which one is current.

Now imagine you're trying to manage 500 employees, track inventory across multiple locations, and handle correspondence with customers in twelve states. Your entire business runs on paper, and that paper is scattered across dozens of shoals, each one organized according to its keeper's personal quirks. Welcome to the information nightmare that was American business in the 1890s.

Enter Edwin G. Seibels, a South Carolina insurance executive with a luxuriant mustache and a penchant for order. In 1898, he invented what would become the most important piece of office furniture in history: the vertical filing cabinet. (Seibels applied for a patent, but it was denied.) Not the horizontal file box that businesses had been using for decades, but a tall, narrow cabinet where documents hung vertically from metal tabs, each one clearly labeled and instantly accessible.

It sounds almost ridiculous today, but Seibels' invention was really revolutionary. Now any document could be filed in a standardized location and retrieved by anyone who knew the system. No more asking around. No more personal hoards of critical information. No more losing track of important papers because they were buried forgotten in a desk drawer.

What we have here is no less than the origin story of the business information system. Before Seibels, the clerk who kept the paper held disproportionate power; after, we saw externalized memory become permanent, standardized – no longer tethered to an individual.

I get pretty excited about things like this.

Within a few decades, every major corporation in America had adopted vertical filing, relegating the pigeonhole desk to the dusty basement. Melvil Dewey—the inventor of the Dewey Decimal System for libraries—also played a big role with his Library Bureau company, which promoted standardized organizational principles across both libraries and offices. The software to Seibels' hardware. Companies developed their own elaborate filing schemes: customers alphabetically, vendors by category, contracts by date, personnel records by department. Each document had its proper place, and anyone could find it as long as they "knew the system."

The filing cabinet didn't just organize information – it organized *people*. Once there was a standardized system for storing and retrieving documents, there was inevitably demand for people to maintain that system, just like at the Library of Alexandria. The filing clerk became an essential role in every organization; not just people who put papers away, they were the guardians of organizational memory.

By the way, if you haven't seen *Desk Set* (Hepburn and Tracy, 1957), you really should.

Office work, as we know it today, was born from the filing cabinet. The name of the "white-collar worker" — someone whose job centered around information rather than physical production — was coined by Upton Sinclair in the 1930s, but the role itself emerged directly from the need to manage all these documents. Filing clerks, stenographers, bookkeepers, and office managers all existed to serve the machine of externalized business memory.

Meanwhile, something else was going on. As companies got more complex, they found that different types of information required different types of expertise. Customer files needed people who understood sales patterns and client behavior. Financial records required specialists in the new cost-accounting methods. Legal documents demanded expertise in contracts and emerging antitrust law. Personnel files needed people who could navigate labor relations and union negotiations. Each domain developed its own specialists, its own knowledge base, its own organizational territory..

Professional specialization followed naturally. If you're the person who understands customer files, you become the customer records specialist. If you're the one who knows the legal filing system, you become the legal clerk. Each specialized filing system created its own specialized role, and each specialized role became the foundation for what would eventually become entire departments, certification programs, advanced degrees, and careers.

The filing cabinet created the modern corporate org chart. Different types of information required different types of expertise, and different types of expertise required different organizational structures. The company that once operated as a single unit with information scattered across individuals became a collection of specialized departments, each with its own filing system, its own expertise, and its own organizational identity.

By 1920, the transformation was largely complete. The typical large corporation looked almost nothing like its 1890s predecessor; instead of a loose collection of individuals managing (or not!) their own information, it was a bureaucratic machine with specialized departments, standardized procedures, and centralized record-keeping.[1]

This wasn't just an American phenomenon. The vertical filing system spread globally, and with it came the organizational structures it enabled. The modern office, with its departments and hierarchies and specialized roles, became *the* way of organizing human economic activity. All because someone figured out how to hang documents vertically instead of stacking them horizontally.

Once businesses had organized their information, there was no going back. But as companies grew larger and their information needs became more complex, the simple elegance of hanging folders started to show its limitations. You can only subdivide so many

---

1. Of course the transformation of the corporation was not exclusively a function of information management. For example, *scientific management* principles, popularized by Frederick Taylor in the 1880s and 1890s and reaching peak influence in the 1910s, added fuel to the shift toward systematic organization and professional management. Taylor was the original guy-with-stopwatch-and-clipboard.

subcategories before the system becomes unwieldy, only store so many documents before retrieval starts to look like rummaging.

Here's a fun fact: the availability of organized information *creates* demand for more information and more sophistication. James Beniger, in "The Control Revolution," says that this isn't accidental—it's the natural evolution of what he called the "crisis of control." As organizations process more energy and materials, they inevitably require more sophisticated information systems in order to maintain control.

Meet Herman Hollerith, a statistician working for the U.S. Census Bureau in the 1880s. Faced with the titanic task of processing the 1890 census, Hollerith realized that the traditional method of hand-tabulating data would take years—possibly longer than the decade between censuses. His solution was another one of those seismic innovations: encode information as holes punched in specific patterns on cards, then use mechanical readers to count and sort the cards automatically.

Hollerith's punch card system wasn't just faster than manual counting—it was exponentially faster. The 1890 population tabulation was completed in just 2½ years compared to the eight years the 1880 census had required. More importantly, the punch cards could be sorted, resorted, and cross-tabulated in ways that manual systems never could. You could ask questions like "How many unmarried women between ages 20-30 live in urban areas?" and get an answer in hours rather than weeks.

The business world took notice immediately. Hollerith and his employees at the Tabulating Machine Company developed punch card systems for commercial enterprises, particularly railroads, which needed to track (heh) complex scheduling and freight information. By the 1920s, punch card systems had evolved beyond simple counting to include basic arithmetic operations, and they were handling payroll, inventory, and customer records for major corporations. Companies like Remington Rand and IBM (which grew out of Hollerith's original company) were selling millions of cards and thousands of machines to businesses hungry for better ways to organize their exploding stores of information.

But punch cards, revolutionary as they were, still operated on the same fundamental principle as the filing cabinet: each piece of information lived in a discrete, physical location. A punch card was essentially a manila folder that machines could read - you still had to know where to look for information, and you still had to organize everything according to pre-determined categories.

Edgar F. Codd was a computer scientist at IBM in 1970 when he published "A Relational Model of Data for Large Shared Data Banks." Codd's insight was elegantly simple and equally radical: instead of storing information in predetermined hierarchical structures, organize it in "tables" where any piece of data could be related to any other piece through shared attributes.

In Codd's *relational* model, you didn't need to know where information was stored, you just needed to know what you were looking for. Want to find all customers who bought product X in the last six months? The database could connect the customer table, the product table, and the sales table to give you the answer.

For the first time, the physical organization of information was completely separated from its logical organization. Data could be stored however was most efficient for the computer, while users could - in theory - access it however made most sense for their work.

Businesses embraced relational databases with growing enthusiasm throughout the 1980s and 1990s. Oracle introduced the first commercial relational database in 1979, followed by IBM's DB2 in 1983. The 1990s brought client-server computing and the World

Wide Web. Major corporations began standardizing on database systems for financial records, manufacturing data, and personnel information. Customer relationship management, enterprise resource planning, human resources management—all of it became database-driven. The database became the new filing cabinet, and the database administrator became the new file clerk.

But here's the rub: databases didn't end up eliminating the organizational thinking that filing cabinets had created. They reinforced it Relational databases still require you to decide, in advance, exactly what categories of information you want to store, and exactly how they related to each other. Before you could put a single piece of data into a database, you had to create a "schema"— a digital blueprint that specified every table, every field, every relationship. The schema was the database equivalent of a filing system's organizational plan. This meant that databases, for all their power and flexibility, *necessarily reflected the processes and habits of the designer* — and the designer had gained all his experience in the era of the filing cabinet, so the database he designed still reflected the same categorical thinking that had shaped business organization since the 1890s.

The schema requirement created something else, too: the need for knowledge workers with elevated specialization. Someone had to design the schemas, and maintain them, and keep them up to date with the business. The database didn't eliminate the clerical function—it elevated it to a technical specialty requiring years of training. Database administration became a profession unto itself, with its own certifications, conferences, lingo, and career paths.

This is exactly what our economist friend Coase predicted—the filing cabinet reduced the transaction costs of internal coordination, enabling companies to grow larger than ever before; databases allowed even larger, more distributed organizations by making information sharing more efficient. But both technologies reinforced the same basic organizational principle: *companies exist to manage information flows that would be too costly to coordinate through market mechanisms.*

As companies grew more sophisticated, they started wanting to connect their databases. Customer information needed to talk to inventory systems. Sales data needed to integrate with financial reporting, and supply chain management needed to coordinate with manufacturing schedules. But each system had been designed with its own schema, its own logic, and its own assumptions about how information should be formatted and organized.

The result was "integration" projects—tedious, expensive efforts to build bridges between incompatible systems. Companies spent millions of dollars and years of effort trying to make their customer database talk to their accounting database, or their inventory system work with their sales system - and an entire industry of consultants and software vendors emerged to solve these integration challenges. Enterprise software companies like SAP, Oracle, and Microsoft built billion-dollar businesses around the promise of unified systems that could handle all of a company's information needs in one integrated platform.

The bigger and more complex these database systems became, the more they reinforced the organizational structures they were supposed to serve. If you had a customer database, you had a customer service department to manage it. The technology and the organization co-evolved, each shaping the other.

By the early 2000s, the modern corporation was, in a very real way, a collection of databases with humans attached. Every department was defined by the specialized information it managed; the filing cabinet had become a sprawling, interconnected network of digital filing cabinets, but the underlying logic remained unchanged. Each department maintained its specialized information processing role, just as Coase and Williamson would have predicted.

It's not immediately intuitive how completely one innovation in information storage—that simple vertical filing cabinet—had reshaped the entire business world and continues to shape it through every subsequent technological evolution.[2] But that's the thing about externalized memory: change how you store information, and you change everything else that depends on that information. The filing cabinet didn't just give us better organization. It gave us the modern corporation, the white-collar workforce, and the bureaucratic structures that still define how we work today.

2. Including, of course, the vestigial symbols and semantics of data storage in the computer world; files, folders, archives.

Chapter Four

THE INFORMATION-COMMERCIAL COMPLEX

It happened at FoxMeyer Drugs in 1995: a $65 million bet on an SAP system to revolutionize the company's daily order volume that instead triggered the destruction of the $5 billion company.

FoxMeyer was one of America's largest pharmaceutical distributors, serving thousands of hospitals, clinics, and drugstores across the country. They had hired SAP (the most established enterprise software company in the world) and Andersen Consulting (the most prestigious systems integrator money could buy). They had deep pockets, experienced management, and a clear business case for why they needed to overhaul their information systems.

The "Delta III" project was to be their digital transformation success story. SAP R/3 would handle all their pharmaceutical ordering and distribution; a new warehouse automation system would manage inventory. Andersen's consultants would integrate everything into one seamless operation that could process millions of orders faster and more efficiently than ever before.

You guessed it: what they got instead was a system that couldn't handle their transaction volumes, couldn't integrate with their existing operations, and couldn't deliver orders reliably. The automation system had bugs on top of bugs that hundreds of workers had to work around manually. Orders were processed incorrectly. Inventory went missing. Customer service was quickly overwhelmed, and collapsed.

By 1996, FoxMeyer had filed for bankruptcy and the CEO had been forced to resign. The company that had spent $65 million to become more efficient had been destroyed by the very system meant to save it. Two years later, FoxMeyer's bankruptcy trustee sued both SAP and Andersen Consulting for $500 million each.

By the early 2000s, pretty much every large corporation had become a collection of incompatible databases, each one a digital fortress protecting its department's way of understanding the business. The corporate database system had promised to eliminate information silos; instead, it had made them permanent.

Hershey's discovered this the hard way in 1999. The chocolate manufacturer decided to implement SAP R/3, supply chain management software, and customer relationship management systems all at once, with a go-live date right before Halloween—their busiest selling season of the year.

Don't do that.

When the systems failed to integrate properly, Hershey's couldn't fulfill orders during the most critical period in their business calendar. The stock price dropped 8%. Revenue plummeted. All because their digital transformation had turned into digital paralysis at exactly the wrong moment.

These weren't isolated incidents. By the early 2000s, something sinister had happened to the relationship between businesses and their information systems.

Our friend the filing cabinet, for all its limitations, had been very flexible. If market conditions changed and you needed to reorganize your business, you bought new folders, made new labels, and moved the files around. The physical reorganization took a few weeks, and you were done. With databases, reorganization became a multi-million-dollar software project. The schemas—those digital blueprints that defined how information could be stored and connected—had become more rigid than any filing system had ever been, and changing them meant changing not just the database structure, but all the applications that depended on it, all the reports that managers relied on, and the tangle of business processes that had grown up around them.

Companies found themselves making business decisions based on what their database systems could handle rather than what the market required. Product lines were organized around existing data categories rather than customer needs, sales territories were drawn to match database segmentation. Pricing strategies were vetoed because of the the limitations of billing systems. The database had become more than just a tool for storing information—it had become a dragon on a chain.

In 1998, SAP had a problem. They had built the most successful enterprise software in the world, but their customers kept asking for features that didn't exist yet. SAP R/3 could handle manufacturing, finance, and human resources beautifully—as long as you were willing to reorganize your entire business around how SAP expected those functions would work. But what if you needed customer relationship management? Supply chain optimization? Business intelligence? E-commerce integration?

SAP's answer: they wouldn't build those features. Instead, they would create an ecosystem of "solution partners" who would build complementary software that *integrated* with R/3. Companies would compete to solve the problems that SAP didn't want to solve directly. What resulted was a "partner ecosystem" that became bigger than SAP itself— and that ecosystem had *a vested interest in keeping things complicated.*

Williamson built on Ronald Coase's "transaction costs"—basically all of the time, money, and hassle it takes to coordinate work between different groups. When companies couldn't get their various software systems to work together, that created huge coordination headaches. But those headaches became goldmines for consulting firms like Accenture, Deloitte, and IBM who built massive, profitable practices around one simple problem: business software systems were terrible at talking to each other.

Today, the global IT consulting market alone represents over $110 billion annually, roughly 20% of the entire $300 billion management consulting industry. Accenture reported $64.9 billion in revenue in 2024, and Deloitte's global revenues exceeded $63 billion that year. These companies didn't just benefit from complexity—they have become economically dependent on it.

The Information-Commercial Complex had perfected the art of artificial scarcity—making abundant information artificially difficult to access and manage. The result was vendor lock-in that transcended technical dependencies. Companies weren't just dependent on software platforms—they were addicted to entire ecosystems of specialized knowledge, certified experts, and approved vendors. Switching databases meant not just migrating data, but rebuilding organizational capabilities, retraining staff, and finding new integration partners who understood the replacement technology.

Williamson's framework perfectly predicted this: instead of reducing coordination costs, the enterprise software industry had discovered how to profit by increasing them. What he couldn't have predicted was how completely this logic would be perverted by the database industry. Instead of using technology to reduce coordination costs, the enterprise software industry had discovered how to profit by *increasing* them.

The Information-Commercial Complex had become self-perpetuating.

The scale of this complex is a little staggering. By the 2000s, the average company was spending over 8% of all its income on information technology. This meant that many companies were spending more money trying to manage their computer systems than they spent creating new products or improving their services. The global market for business software had ballooned to over $900 billion a year by the 2020s. This wasn't just companies buying useful technology—it was feeding the monster that kept their data trapped in separate, incompatible systems.

UPS discovered that their own internal data systems were so disconnected that they couldn't answer basic operational questions without substantial integration projects. Customer data lived in one system, package tracking in another, route optimization in a third, and billing in a fourth. The company's 'solution' perfectly illustrates the Information-Commercial Complex at work: instead of questioning why these systems couldn't talk to each other, they spent hundreds of millions of dollars and four years building ORION—yet another layer of complexity on top of the complexity they already had.

To be sure, ORION saved 100 million miles of driving annually. But the 'success' locked UPS into maintaining ORION plus all their legacy systems for decades. The integration project that was supposed to solve their problems became another system that would need its own integration projects. They celebrated solving the symptom while institutionalizing the disease.

This is the specter of the Information-Commercial Complex. Every player has reasonable technical reasons for making things complicated, and the cost simplification gets more prohibitive with every step. Database companies built adaptable systems that needed expensive specialists to set up properly. Consulting firms developed detailed processes that turned straightforward problems into complex, lengthy projects. IT service providers created custom solutions that couldn't be easily automated or turned into standard products. Internal IT departments selected different systems that required careful planning to work together. Each group was making sensible decisions based on their own interests.

The problem wasn't that anybody was acting maliciously; the problem was that everyone's economic incentives were aligned to maintain complexity rather than eliminate it.

This is "institutional lock-in," when the rules of the game become so entrenched that changing them is prohibitively expensive, even when everyone agrees the current rules are suboptimal. The Information-Commercial Complex had achieved a perfect institutional lock-in: every major participant had made investments that would lose value if the system became simpler. The database vendors had built product lines around complexity. The consulting firms had built methodologies around long-term engagements. The IT professionals had built careers around specialized knowledge.

Universities and certification programs had created a self-reinforcing professional culture that perpetuated the Complex. Computer science graduates who spent years learning Oracle database administration or SAP implementation methodology naturally gravitated toward jobs where they could apply that hard-earned knowledge. Once hired, they had professional incentives to choose technologies that validated their expertise rather than simpler alternatives that might make their skills obsolete. These professionals in turn became the hiring managers and technical leaders who made purchasing decisions for the next generation of enterprise software; having invested years mastering complex systems, they were committed to believing that enterprise-grade problems required enterprise-grade solutions, and they hired people who shared their technical background and promoted colleagues who demonstrated mastery of the same complex systems they themselves had learned.

This is what sociologists call "social reproduction"—the way each generation of IT leaders taught the next generation to approach problems using the same methods, ensuring that demand for complex, specialized solutions would persist even when simpler options became available. Pierre Bourdieu called it *habitus*; the deeply ingrained dispositions, tastes, and ways of thinking that professionals develop through their training and practice.

Basically, successful professionals had too much invested in the status quo to seriously consider alternatives.

The Information-Commercial Complex had become the economy's largest *rent-seeking operation*—a system that extracts money without creating equivalent value in return. Companies were employing more database administrators, systems analysts, and integration specialists than they had product engineers, customer service representatives, or salespeople. The infrastructure for managing information had grown larger than the infrastructure for actually creating value.

Changing any of it required changing all of it, and changing all of it was so expensive, so risky, and so disruptive that most companies don't even consider it. They learned to live within the constraints of systems that had been built fto solve problems that no longer existed.The database had achieved something the filing cabinet never could: it had made organizational change economically impossible.

But rent-seeking operations, no matter how entrenched, are vulnerable to technological disruption *if it eliminates the scarcity they depend on*. The participants in the Information-Commercial Complex had built their business models around the assumption that managing enterprise information requires specialized knowledge, elaborate integration projects, and expensive ongoing maintenance.

We're about to discover what happens when those assumptions become obsolete. The question isn't whether someone would build information systems that didn't require an Information-Commercial Complex to operate. The question was what would happen to all the participants in the Complex when they did.

Chapter Five

DIFFERENT RULES ENTIRELY

A team of eight scientists at Google published a research paper in 2017 called "Attention Is All You Need." It's a dry, technical paper about neural network architectures, the kind of thing that normally gets read by a other researchers and then forgotten. But this paper introduced something called the "Transformer" - a new way of building systems that could understand and generate human language.

The paper has since been cited more than 173,000 times, placing it among the top ten most-cited papers of the 21st century. Within five years, that paper had spawned ChatGPT, Claude, Gemini, Copilot, and dozens of others - and a revolution that's about to make the structured database obsolete. These systems didn't just master *language*—they revealed something about information itself. By learning to predict the next word in billions of sentences, they developed an ability to understand meaning and relationships in any kind of data. The same mathematical approach that lets ChatGPT write poetry can help businesses understand customer behavior, detect fraud patterns, or predict equipment failures. The breakthrough wasn't just in processing language; it was in discovering that all information—text, numbers, images, patterns—can be understood through the same mathematical framework.

What we presently call "AI" is going to be woven into everything, the way that the internet is now; once a novelty, now a utility. AI represents a whole new way to store, synthesize, and retrieve information that doesn't require a person to speak computerese, because the computer can speak human… -ese. You know what I'm saying.

AI systems can work with information in its natural, unstructured form. Where traditional databases require you to know exactly what you're looking for and how it's organized, AI systems can understand what you mean and find what you need. Most importantly, where databases require an entire Information-Commercial Complex to implement and maintain, AI systems can be deployed by a single person with a laptop.

We're about to discover what happens when the fundamental constraints that created the modern corporation disappear.

Instead of organizing information into rigid categories, AIs represent everything as "vectors" - essentially, lists of numbers that capture the meaning of, and relationships between, pieces of information. When an AI system encounters a piece of text, an image, or any other kind of information, it converts that information into a mathematical representation that captures its essential meaning. Similar concepts end up with similar mathematical representations; related ideas cluster together in this mathematical space.

If you had to represent every word in the English language as a point on a map, words with similar meanings would end up close to each other. "Cat" and "dog" would be near each other in the "pet" neighborhood. "Love" and "affection" would be close in the "emotion" district. "Database" and "spreadsheet" would be neighbors in "business software" territory.

The AI figures out these relationships automatically by analyzing oceans of text, and learning the patterns of how words and concepts relate to each other. You don't have to tell it that cats and dogs are both pets, or that love and affection are similar emotions. It discovers these relationships by reading millions of documents and noticing how these words tend to appear in similar contexts. This means you can store information in its natural form - emails, documents, chat logs, images, audio recordings - and the AI can understand the relationships and meanings without you having to organize everything into predefined categories first.

In the financial sector, banks are using AI systems to detect fraud by representing transaction patterns as vectors. Instead of writing rules for every possible fraudulent scenario (which was the traditional approach), the AI learns what normal and abnormal transaction patterns look like and can identify suspicious activity even when it doesn't match any previously known fraud pattern. Spotify uses vector databases to power its search and recommendation functions, and Facebook's facial recognition system converts facial features into mathematical vectors, rather than storing specific measurements in predefined field, allowing it to recognize faces in different lighting conditions, angles, and expressions.

When an AI system needs information, it can query multiple databases, documents, emails, chat logs, and any other source of information, understand the relationships between all of these different data sources, and provide a coherent answer: no integration project required. This isn't just more convenient - it's a sea change in how information systems work. Remember all those clerical workers whose jobs existed primarily to move information between systems, organize it according to predetermined categories, and format it for different purposes? AI systems can do most of that work automatically.

Example: financial analysts who spend their time pulling data from multiple systems, formatting it consistently and creating reports simply won't need to do that anymore. They can ask a question like "Why did our Northeast region outperform the budget by 12% last quarter?" and get a comprehensive answer that draws from sales data, customer feedback, market conditions, competitor actions, internal operational metrics, and even weather patterns. The AI can access all these different sources of information, understand the relationships between them, and provide insights that might have taken a team of analysts weeks to compile. Then, they can ask follow-up questions: "Which specific product lines drove that outperformance?" "How much of this was due to the new marketing campaign versus external market factors?" "Should we expect this trend to continue next quarter?" Each question builds on the previous answers, creating a natural conversation rather than a series of separate reporting requests.

The transformation extends beyond analysis into operational tasks. Instead of maintaining complex workflows to route customer service tickets through multiple systems, an AI can understand a customer complaint, automatically gather relevant account history, identify similar issues, suggest solutions based on past resolutions, and even draft personalized responses that account for the customer's communication style and relationship history with the company.

This brings us to the biggest implication of the shift from databases to AI, and the central thesis of this book: the elimination of artificial scarcity in information management.

The Information-Commercial Complex that we explored earlier is built on the premise that managing enterprise information required specialized knowledge, elaborate systems, and expensive ongoing maintenance. Database vendors, systems integrators, and consulting firms all profited from the complexity that made their expertise essential.

But AI systems eliminate most of this complexity. When information can be stored in its natural form, when systems can understand meaning rather than requiring predefined structures, when deployment takes hours instead of months, the specialized knowledge that justified the entire ecosystem becomes moot. This doesn't mean that all information management becomes trivial - there are still important questions about data quality, security, and governance. But the pitfalls and barriers that made corporate information systems so expensive and difficult to implement are disappearing .

The transformation echoes the shift from filing cabinets to databases, but in reverse. Where databases created new forms of complexity that required specialized expertise to manage, AI systems reduce complexity and make sophisticated information management accessible to non-specialists. Where the filing cabinet enabled the first large corporations by making information management scalable, and databases enabled even larger, more distributed organizations by making information sharing more efficient, AI systems will enable smaller, more agile, low-drag organizations to operate at a global scale.

The question isn't whether this transformation will happen - the technology is already here and improving rapidly. What we breathlessly call "AI" now will soon just be *how things work*. It's not that the rules of the game are changing - it's a different game altogether.

To understand what this transformation means for organizations, we need to examine how corporations organize and use their information today. The structures weren't arbitrary—they evolved for specific reasons, served real purposes, and created the entire organizational reality we take for granted. Once we see how completely our corporations depend on information living in separate, incompatible categories, we'll understand why the ability to connect everything changes everything.

Chapter Six

THE THREE TYPES OF CORPORATE MEMORY

Walk into any large corporation's headquarters and ask to see everything they know about a single customer. Not just purchase history or support tickets—everything across all systems and departments.

What you'll discover is corporate schizophrenia at scale. The sales system knows the customer bought licenses three years ago but doesn't know they've called support forty-seven times. The support system knows every ticket but can't see they're sixty days late on payment. Finance knows about the late payment but has no idea the customer is the CEO's college roommate, recorded only in someone's email. Strategic planning has identified the customer's industry as a growth target but doesn't know the customer is about to switch to a competitor.

This isn't incompetence. It's the inevitable result of how we've organized corporate information for the past half-century.

In 1965, management theorist Robert Anthony published what became known as the Anthony Triangle (though it's really more of a pyramid). Working from Harvard Business School, Anthony watched corporations struggle with early computers and divided management into three levels. At the top sat Strategic Planning, where executives made long-term decisions about market positioning and resource allocation. In the middle was Management Control, where managers monitored performance and coordinated operations. At the bottom was Operational Control, where supervisors handled daily tasks and transactions.

Each level, Anthony observed, needs very different information. Strategic planners want broad trends and future projections, often qualitative and external-facing. Middle managers need performance metrics and budget variances, comparing actual to planned performance. Operations needs real-time transaction data, specific and immediate. It seemed logical enough, and for sixty years, it's been gospel in enterprise software design.

What Anthony didn't, couldn't have predicted was that his information framework would calcify into rigid organizational structures whose incentives ran counter to the core of the business, and every enterprise software company took the pyramid as divine truth. SAP built separate modules for strategic, tactical, and operational users; Oracle created different databases for different organizational levels; IBM sold different systems to different departments.

Anecdotes of Boeing's 787 Dreamliner disaster perfectly illustrate Anthony's tragedy. The company's *operational* systems were screaming about battery problems—quality control had documented anomalies in power output and heat generation, test engineers had filed reports about thermal runaway risks, and suppliers had flagged concerns about battery chemistry. All this critical information was trapped at the bottom of Anthony's pyramid, dutifully filed in operational databases where it "belonged." Meanwhile, executives at the strategic level were making design decisions in blissful ignorance, separated from the warning signs by layers of organizational hierarchy and incompatible information systems. Each piece of data stayed at its designated level, unable to climb fast enough to matter. By the time the full picture reached the top of the pyramid, planes were grounded worldwide and billions were lost. The information that could have prevented the catastrophe existed all along—it just couldn't travel between organizational levels fast enough to save Boeing from itself.

Anthony's framework assumes information naturally belongs at certain organizational levels, but information doesn't respect boundaries. A customer complaint might be operational data to the service rep handling the call, management information to the department head tracking satisfaction metrics, and strategic intelligence to the CEO wondering about product-market fit. The same piece of information has different meanings at different levels, but schemas and *habitus* make us choose one home for it, creating blind spots at every level.

Target discovered this when they wanted to identify pregnant customers—famously, to market baby products at the perfect moment. The data they needed was scattered across dozens of systems built according to Anthony's hierarchy. Purchase history lived in operational databases, demographic data in management systems, browsing behavior in marketing analytics, payment methods in financial systems. The project to combine this information took years and millions of dollars, not because the analysis was complex, but because the information lived in separate universes that spoke different languages, each one believing it owned the "correct" view of the customer.

Then came the fourth layer that Anthony never anticipated: regulatory compliance. After Enron collapsed and WorldCom imploded and nearly broke the global economy, regulations like Sarbanes-Oxley and Dodd-Frank created an entirely new category of information demand. This wasn't strategic planning, management control, or operational execution—it was pure retention for retention's sake. Companies now maintain vast digital mausoleums of information serving no business purpose except satisfying regulators who might ask for it someday.

Major banks routinely report spending hundreds of millions annually on compliance data storage and management. Bank of America, for instance, disclosed compliance costs exceeding $2 billion annually, with a significant portion dedicated to data retention systems that serve no business purpose beyond regulatory satisfaction. This information sits frozen in amber, indexed and searchable but never accessed, waiting for regulators who might never come knocking.

While Anthony's framework helped us understand management levels, the reality of modern corporate information requires a different lens. Instead of organizing by hierarchy, we need to understand information by its fundamental purpose. *Decision Support* Information exists to make humans smarter—the market research, competitive intelligence, and customer analytics we collect specifically to improve judgment and strategic choices. This is the realm of PowerPoints and Excel models, of consultants and strategy meetings, of asking "what if?" and "why not?"

Operational Feedback Information exists to keep the machine running—the system logs, quality metrics, and performance indicators that tell us whether things are working. This is the realm of dashboards and alerts, of monitoring systems and exception reports, of asking "is everything okay?" every second of every day.

Regulatory Retention Information exists to keep us out of jail—the financial records, audit trails, and compliance documentation we maintain because someone with a badge and a subpoena might ask for it. This is the realm of archives and retention policies, of compliance officers and external auditors, of proving we did what we said we did when we said we did it.

These three purposes require different approaches to information lifecycle management. Decision support information needs to be flexible and combinable, operational feedback needs to be real-time and actionable, regulatory retention needs to be immutable and comprehensive. But—and here's where Anthony's framework breaks down completely—they don't require separate systems. That's just an artifact of our technological limitations. The same information serves all three purposes simultaneously, but our databases can't handle that complexity, so we duplicate everything, creating the sprawling clerical infrastructure we explored earlier.

As we've seen throughout this book, AI systems process information differently than databases. When a customer complains on social media about a product defect, traditional systems would route this to customer service as an operational issue. But an AI system reading that same complaint converts it into a mathematical representation—a vector—that captures not just the words but their meaning and context. That vector naturally relates to other vectors in the system: previous complaints about similar issues, quality control reports from manufacturing, sales patterns showing returns, even regulatory requirements about product safety disclosures.

The AI doesn't consciously decide "this is operational and strategic and compliance-related." Instead, the mathematical relationships between vectors reveal these connections automatically. The complaint vector sits close to other urgent customer service issues in one dimension (operational), clusters with product quality patterns in another dimension (strategic), and maps to required disclosure protocols in a third dimension (regulatory). When the system queries for "what needs immediate attention," the complaint appears. When it queries for "product quality trends," the same complaint appears. When it queries for "regulatory reporting requirements," there it is again. Same information, multiple contexts, no human translation required.

This isn't science fiction—it's how vector databases and semantic search work today. Companies like Spotify use this to understand that a song is simultaneously dance music, workout music, and 90s nostalgia, without maintaining three separate categorization systems. The same mathematical principles that let Netflix understand that a show appeals to both true crime fans and documentary lovers can let businesses understand that a customer complaint is both an operational fire to put out and strategic intelligence about product design.

The companies that understand this will stop organizing information by level or purpose or department. They'll let information flow through vector spaces where meaning and relationships emerge naturally from the mathematics rather than from predetermined categories. The ones that don't will maintain their careful taxonomies and their pyramid structures right up until a competitor using vector-based systems eats their lunch by understanding patterns they never saw coming.

The pyramid served us well when information was scarce and processing power was limited. But in an age of infinite storage and AI that can process all information simultaneously, maintaining Anthony's boundaries isn't just inefficient—it's corporate suicide in slow motion. The question isn't whether to abandon the pyramid, but whether you'll jump off it or be buried under it when it falls.

Chapter Seven

ALL TOGETHER, NOW

There's a *convergence* happening right now that's erasing the information boundaries that created the modern corporation. For over a century, as we've seen, companies organized around three distinct types of information—Decision Support, Operational Feedback, and Regulatory Retention— and beyond that developed a self-reinforcing system of clerical specialists in different fields.

AI-type systems don't need these distinctions, and are in fact hindered by the gaps that they create - but the removal of these cornerstones will lead to the collapse of the organizational design they've supported for generations.

Traditional databases require information to be categorized before it can be stored: customer data goes in customer tables, financial data goes in financial tables, etc. Each category requires different schemas, different access controls, and different expertise to maintain.

AI systems work through *semantic representation*, converting all information into mathematical vectors that capture meaning and relationships. A customer complaint, a financial transaction, and a compliance audit all become points in the same mathematical space, where their relationships and patterns emerge naturally without human categorization.

This, right here, is the game changer — not the resulting ability to write articles, or make fake videos of celebrities, *but the very different way of viewing data in relation to other data.* When you force AI to respect traditional information silos, you're essentially asking it to ignore valuable patterns that traverse those boundaries.

Netflix demonstrates this perfectly. When their system notices that users who watch Korean dramas also engage heavily with cooking shows, that's not a business intelligence report generated by analysts—it's immediate strategic intelligence emerging directly from viewing behavior. The AI doesn't distinguish between operational data (what people watch) and strategic insight (what content to develop). It sees patterns that suggest business opportunities instantly.

The same convergence is happening everywhere AI systems are deployed. Mayo Clinic's AI systems monitoring patient outcomes don't just improve treatment protocols—they automatically generate documentation for regulatory reporting while identifying patterns that inform strategic planning about facility expansion. JPMorgan Chase's COIN system processes commercial loan agreements in seconds rather than requiring 360,000 hours of lawyer time, but it doesn't just ensure compliance—it identifies risk patterns that inform lending strategy, spots emerging market opportunities, and optimizes operational workflows simultaneously.

Here's what all these companies are discovering at once: when AI can see all the patterns all the time, the old rhythms of business quickly become absurd.

The most immediate organizational impact is the collapse of planning cycles. When strategic intelligence emerges automatically from operational data, the quarterly business review becomes obsolete. Convergent organizations detect market changes as they happen; every customer interaction, every operational metric, and every external signal becomes immediate strategic intelligence without waiting for reports or meetings. Netflix doesn't wait for quarterly viewer surveys to understand changing preferences. They see shifting patterns in real-time and can greenlight new content while competitors are still analyzing last quarter's data. The speed advantage compounds over time.

Organizations with real-time strategic intelligence make dozens of small competitive moves while traditional competitors prepare for their next planning cycle - and they have no use for departmental information ownership. When AI systems can understand all types of information using the same mathematical principles, departmental specialization becomes a barrier to value creation rather than an enabler. Marketing departments analyzing customer data in isolation can't see how preferences relate to production constraints, supply chain costs, or regulatory changes. An AI system analyzing all data simultaneously identifies opportunities that no departmental specialist could discover.

This creates convergence pressure—organizations maintaining artificial boundaries can't compete with those that have eliminated them, and the competitive disadvantage isn't subtle, it's dramatic and immediate. A traditional retailer analyzing seasonal patterns might take weeks to coordinate insights across departments. A convergent retailer's AI analyzes everything simultaneously and continuously—patterns emerge as they happen, inventory adjusts automatically, pricing strategies adapt in real-time.

But adaptation isn't uniform, and the human cost isn't abstract.

We're talking about the potential displacement of millions of people who currently make their living managing information complexity. In the United States alone, based on Bureau of Labor Statistics numbers, there are roughly 4.6 million administrative workers, 1.4 million bookkeeping clerks, 700,000 HR specialists, and countless others whose primary function is serving as human bridges between incompatible systems. These aren't statistics—they're people with mortgages, families, and decades of specialized knowledge.

The cruelest irony is that the most diligent workers—those who mastered Oracle databases, became SAP certified, or learned regulatory compliance—will be hit hardest. Their expertise in navigating artificial complexity becomes a liability when that complexity evaporates. It's very much like being an accomplished telegraph operator in 1876, the year Alexander Graham Bell patented the telephone.

Financial services will likely experience convergence first and most dramatically. Banks already operate almost entirely in the digital realm. When JPMorgan's COIN system reviews loan agreements in seconds instead of requiring thousands of lawyer hours, we're not looking at improvement—we're looking at elimination of entire departments. A bank that achieves convergence can offer better rates, faster service, and superior risk assessment while operating at a fraction of traditional costs.

Healthcare presents a different picture. While diagnostic AI outperforms human radiologists in many contexts, the sector's transformation will be slowed by legitimate safety concerns and the irreducibly human aspects of care. You can't automate empathy. But even healthcare's slower transformation will be traumatic. Medical coding, insurance processing, appointment scheduling—these administrative functions employ millions and could largely disappear. The average hospital spends 25% of its budget on administration. When AI eliminates the need for armies translating between insurance systems and hospital records, those jobs don't transform—they vanish.

Manufacturing will have its revenge, being among the least affected in terms of employment. Factory workers do physical work that AI can't directly replace. Convergence might increase manufacturing employment by making it economical to produce goods closer to consumers.

Government services face unique challenges. Historically in the US, government agencies couldn't simply fire millions when AI makes jobs redundant - though recent actions belie that. The political complexity of mass government layoffs combined with the inertia of governments in general means the public sector will become an employment buffer—a place where artificial complexity is deliberately maintained to preserve jobs. This isn't necessarily bad; gradual transition might be more humane than private sector efficiency. But government services will increasingly lag private alternatives, creating privatization pressure that could ultimately result in even more dramatic losses.

The geographic dimension makes it even more complex. Cities like San Francisco and New York—built on information work—face existential questions. Every high-paying office job supports roughly four to five service jobs: the barista who makes their coffee, the driver who delivers their lunch, the cleaner who maintains their office, the bartender who serves their after-work drinks. When companies need fewer office workers, it's not just those jobs that vanish. What happens to commercial real estate when offices empty? What happens to the tax base when both the high-paying clerical jobs and all the service jobs they supported disappear?[3]

We're about to run a super-sized social experiment with no control group and no ability to stop if things go wrong. Some sectors will transform overnight while others resist for decades, some workers will thrive while others are marginalized, some communities will reinvent themselves while others become monuments to the world that was.

The boundaries that created the modern corporation are dissolving. What emerges will be as different from today's database-driven organizations as they are from the filing cabinet businesses of a century ago. The convergent organization operates more like a biological system than a mechanical one—information flows naturally to where it's needed, decisions emerge from comprehensive understanding rather than

---

3. Meanwhile, smaller cities might actually benefit, as the dispersal of the COVID era gains momentum.

departmental specialization, and adaptation happens continuously rather than through periodic planning cycles. This isn't just organizational change—it's the elimination of artificial constraints on human coordination that have existed since humans organized around information.

The tyranny of the filing cabinet is ending. What replaces it will be more responsive and more intelligent than anything we've seen before – but whether it will be more humane depends entirely on the choices we make during this transition. The technology is neutral—it's our response that will determine whether the filing cabinet created the white-collar middle class only to have AI convergence eliminate it, or whether we find new forms of meaningful work in a converged world.

The question isn't whether convergence will happen—the mathematics and economics make it inevitable. The question is whether we'll handle the transition with wisdom and compassion or let market forces sort winners from losers with brutal efficiency. History suggests we'll muddle through with both—and that muddle will define the next century of human organization.

Chapter Eight

THE RESISTANCE MACHINE

In the previous chapter, we talked about how AI convergence threatens to hollow out the vast clerical infrastructure that has mediated between incompatible information systems for over a century. But our old friend the Information-Commercial Complex —the $700+ billion ecosystem of vendors, consultants, and specialists who profit from information system complexity—will not simply accept obsolescence, and it has both the economic incentives and institutional power to significantly slow AI adoption in the West through regulatory capture, artificial complexity, and professional guild protection, potentially delaying the benefits of convergence by decades while extracting trillions in rent from the global economy.

This isn't a conspiracy theory, it's just economics. When an industry worth hundreds of billions faces technological disruption, it doesn't passively await, much less embrace, displacement – it fights back using every tool at its disposal: lobbying for favorable regulations, designing complexity into new technologies, capturing regulatory agencies, and using professional credentialing to maintain artificial scarcities. The history of technological disruption shows that incumbent industries usually succeed in delaying–if not preventing–transformations that threaten their economic foundations.

Economic historian Joel Mokyr's research on technological resistance shows that incumbent industries have historically been able to delay technological adoption by decades through what he calls "institutional inertia" and "entrenched interests." Mokyr documents how established guilds in medieval Europe successfully resisted labor-saving innovations for centuries, and how similar dynamics operate in modern economies. His work suggests that technological capability alone is insufficient to drive change—institutions and interest groups play decisive roles in determining adoption speed.

The resistance is already underway, though it's often disguised as prudent caution about AI risks, calls for responsible innovation, or concerns about algorithmic bias. While some of these concerns are definitely legitimate, many serve as convenient justifications for preserving the lucrative status quo.

To forecast the intensity of the resistance, we need to appreciate the magnitude of what the Information-Commercial Complex stands to lose.

The global enterprise software market was valued at $264 billion in 2024 and is projected to reach $517 billion by 2030. But those projections *assume continued demand* for complex integration, elaborate customization, and ongoing maintenance — exactly the services that AI convergence threatens to eliminate. **Management consulting**, built largely on helping companies navigate information system complexity, represents approximately $358 billion annually as of 2025. The Big Four consulting firms—Deloitte, PwC, EY, and KPMG—collectively employ over

1.2 million people globally, with much of their revenue derived from enterprise technology implementations, systems integration, and digital transformation projects.

Business process outsourcing, which exists at least in large part because companies can't efficiently manage their own complex information systems, generates over $300 billion in annual revenue as of 2024. Countries like India, Philippines, and Ireland have built significant portions of their economies around managing the complexity that AI convergence could eliminate.

The professional services sector—legal, accounting, financial advisory—has evolved into a massive global industry, with estimates ranging from $1-7 trillion annually (depending on how you slice it). Much of this sector owes its existence to the complexity of navigating incompatible information systems and regulatory frameworks. Law firms bill hundreds of billions annually for document review, compliance consulting, and regulatory interpretation that AI systems could perform more accurately at marginal cost.

In total, we're looking at an ecosystem worth at least $3.5 trillion annually that depends directly on information system complexity—and that's being conservative. Include the indirect costs of inefficiency, the opportunity costs of delayed decisions, and the human capital locked into maintaining these systems, and the real economic impact approaches $5 trillion. That's roughly the GDP of Japan, the world's third-largest economy, devoted entirely to managing artificial complexity.

But the resistance isn't just from faceless corporations and billionaires. Behind those trillions of dollars are people whose mortgages, retirements, and identities depend on the current system's complexity. The database administrator who spent a decade mastering Oracle, the consultant who built her career on SAP implementations, the IT manager whose team exists to maintain integration between systems—they're not just protecting business models, they're protecting their lives. This makes the resistance especially fierce: it's one thing to fight for market share; it's another to fight for your family's future.

The resistance begins with misaligned incentives. Consulting firms bill by the hour, not by outcome—creating obvious incentives to recommend complex solutions over simple ones. Anyone who has paid by the hour for anything understands this immediately.

A project that takes six months generates three times the revenue of one that takes two months, *regardless of the final result.* When McKinsey charges $3.8 million to advise the Postal Service on operational efficiency, or when Deloitte bills $135 million for a failed NHS patient record system, the failures don't reduce profitability—they often increase it by justifying additional consulting phases.

At the same time, enterprise software vendors have discovered that artificial complexity creates more sustainable competitive advantages than genuine innovation. Economic research on platform markets by MIT's David Autor and others shows how incumbent technology firms can create "switching costs" that trap customers in their ecosystems regardless of superior alternatives. Oracle's database licensing model, for example, is so deliberately complex that entire consulting practices exist solely to help companies understand their Oracle licensing obligations. Companies regularly pay millions in "compliance gaps" because Oracle's intentionally confusing licensing terms make it virtually impossible to remain fully compliant.

Oracle and others have discovered that artificial complexity is more profitable than genuine innovation—it creates higher barriers to entry and locks customers in more effectively.

Systems integrators have the strongest incentives to maintain complexity—their entire business model depends on systems remaining incompatible.. Companies like IBM Global Services, Accenture, and Capgemini generate tens of billions annually by serving as intermediaries between systems that could theoretically communicate directly. They've developed proprietary methodologies, specialized frameworks, and custom tools that make clients more dependent on their services rather than less. The integration industry has become expert at "scope creep"—gradually expanding project requirements to justify larger budgets and longer timelines.

Maybe the most sophisticated resistance strategy involves capturing the regulatory apparatus to slow AI adoption through legal requirements for human oversight, complex approval processes, and mandated use of traditional approaches. This is classic regulatory capture—the industries being regulated end up controlling the regulators.

Professional associations have spent decades building legal moats around their expertise. Occupational licensing now covers nearly 25% of U.S. workers compared to 5% in the 1950s, creating legal barriers that prevent AI adoption even when the technology demonstrably outperforms humans. Professional licensing boards maintain their gatekeeping power by mandating human certification—lawyers must review legal documents, doctors must make diagnoses, CPAs must certify financial statements—even when AI outperforms humans at each of these tasks.

Instead of *reducing* human involvement as technology advances, licensing boards frequently add new requirements for human oversight that preserve incumbent employment.

The influence operates through a "revolving door" documented in political economy research. Studies by economists at the National Bureau of Economic Research show that a majority of senior regulators across industries eventually join the private sector companies they once oversaw - and who doesn't want to be nice to their future employer? These *career incentives* can be more powerful than direct lobbying, because they create ongoing relationships and shared interests between regulators and industry participants.

Industry associations sponsor regulatory conferences, fund academic research, and provide "thought leadership" that shapes regulatory thinking. The Software & Information Industry Association, for example, sponsors dozens of regulatory events annually where government officials meet with industry leaders to discuss "appropriate" approaches to technology oversight.

The resistance machine has proven particularly effective at capturing *technical standards development*. Incumbent firms shape technical standards to favor their existing capabilities over superior alternatives. In AI governance, this manifests as elaborate standards for AI testing, certification, and deployment - that favor organizations with existing regulatory expertise.

The IEEE, ISO, and other standards bodies developing AI governance frameworks include heavy representation from incumbent consulting firms and enterprise software vendors. These organizations have strong incentives to develop standards that require professional interpretation and implementation rather than standards that enable simple, direct AI adoption. Complex standards favor large organizations with dedicated compliance teams over smaller competitors with simpler solutions.

The EU AI Act, for example, runs to over 180 pages and requires extensive legal and technical expertise to interpret. This complexity serves incumbent industries perfectly—it doesn't prevent AI adoption, but it ensures that AI adoption requires the same armies of lawyers, consultants, and compliance specialists that traditional technology implementations require.

And then we have the reapplication of the old to the new. Research by economists like David Evans and Richard Schmalensee shows how the established players can extend into new technological domains by forcing new capabilities through existing complex architectures. Microsoft's AI offerings, for example, are deeply integrated into its existing enterprise software ecosystem. Companies can't simply adopt powerful AI capabilities—they have to navigate licensing arrangements, integration requirements, and governance frameworks that preserve Microsoft's platform advantages (and their consulting partners' revenue streams). Research by economists like Carl Shapiro and Hal Varian on "information rules" shows how companies can create artificial switching costs *even in markets with low natural barriers to entry*. AI vendors are applying these strategies by developing proprietary models that create new forms of vendor lock-in.

While Silicon Valley debates AI safety and Brussels drafts 180-page regulations, some tectonic stuff is happening in Shenzhen, Bangalore, and Lagos. Countries that never fully invested in the database-industrial complex are discovering they can skip it entirely.

It's 1990s Kenya all over again. Back then, Kenya had minimal landline infrastructure—a disadvantage that became an advantage when mobile phones arrived. Without legacy copper wire investments to protect, Kenya jumped straight to mobile technology. M-Pesa, the mobile payment system launched in 2007, transformed Kenya into a global leader in financial technology while American banks were still pushing paper checks.

The same leapfrogging is about to happen with AI convergence, but the stakes are a lot higher. Countries and companies without decades of database investments, enterprise software licenses, and armies of IT consultants have nothing to protect: they can adopt convergent AI systems immediately, while Western corporations are still paying off their SAP implementations.

While American companies navigate the Information-Commercial Complex's resistance strategies, Chinese firms are building AI-first organizations from scratch. ByteDance built TikTok with AI at its core from day one—not trying to retrofit AI into existing enterprise architectures. The result? They decoded global consumer attention patterns while Facebook was still trying to migrate Instagram's databases.

The geographic pattern of resistance follows the money. The United States, with its $400 billion enterprise software industry and hundreds of thousands of IT consultants, faces the strongest headwinds. The European Union, addicted to regulatory complexity as a competitive moat, is crafting AI governance frameworks that codify the desires of the resistance machine. Japan, despite its technological prowess, remains imprisoned by corporate cultures that treat information systems as defensive fortifications rather than offensive weapons.

India, the country that built its modern economy on managing the West's database complexity—the entire business process outsourcing industry—faces an existential choice. India could use its deep understanding of Western information systems to accelerate convergence, or it could join the resistance to protect the millions of jobs that depend on artificial complexity. Early signals suggest a split: India's domestic companies are embracing AI convergence while its outsourcing giants are repositioning themselves as "AI transformation consultants"—essentially betting they can manage the transition slowly enough to preserve their business models.

Singapore and the UAE are investing heavily in AI as a national competitive strategy, creating more flexible regulatory environments to attract AI-first companies.

Here's where I get to use the fun phrase "regulatory arbitrage." As different jurisdictions take very different approaches to AI governance—from Europe's comprehensive regulations to Singapore's innovation-friendly policies to the American sector-specific patchwork—companies will inevitably gravitate toward the most favorable environments. We're already seeing AI startups choosing to incorporate outside the EU, and companies establishing development centers in countries with strong technical talent but fewer regulatory constraints. Countries that understand this new geography of innovation are positioning themselves accordingly.

It's regulatory arbitrage, you see. We're about to find out what happens when some economies embrace convergence while others resist it.

History suggests the outcome isn't subtle. When Britain resisted industrial automation to protect textile workers, it didn't stop the Industrial Revolution—it just moved it to America. When Detroit resisted fuel efficiency standards to protect SUV profits, it didn't stop the automotive revolution—it handed it to Toyota and Tesla.

The difference this time is *speed*. The Industrial Revolution took decades to shift economic power from Britain to America. The automotive revolution took years to shift from Detroit to Tokyo and Shanghai. The AI convergence will be measured in quarters, not decades. A company that achieves convergence in 2025 will be competing with such advantages by 2026 that traditionally-organized competitors won't be able to respond. - regardless of their resources or market position.

The likely, and ironic, outcome is that the countries that invested least in 20th-century information technology become the leaders of 21st-century economic organization. The filing cabinet was invented in America and perfected there. The database was invented in America and dominated by American companies. But AI convergence might belong to whoever has the least to lose from abandoning those earlier innovations.

America's Information-Commercial Complex might successfully slow convergence within its borders, but it can't stop it globally. And in a connected world, that might be worse than useless—it would be economic suicide in slow motion.

Recent history provides ample evidence of successful resistance to technological change: financial services delaying electronic trading adoption through regulatory capture in the 1970s; telecommunications industries hampering internet adoption in the 1990s; and healthcare maintaining human oversight requirements for medical technologies even when AI demonstrates superior diagnostic performance.

AI convergence could increase global productivity by 20-40% and add $13 trillion to global output by 2030—but resistance strategies could cut these gains in half while redirecting entrepreneurial energy toward rent-seeking rather than innovation.

However, there's a tipping point. Cost advantages of 50% or more typically overcome regulatory barriers within 5-10 years — and AI systems already demonstrate 80-95% cost advantages for many information processing tasks. International competition means that countries that stick too closely to their regulatory inertia will likely change strategy when other nations start to surpass them.

The battle between AI convergence and the Information-Commercial Complex' resistance will be one for the history books.

Chapter Nine

SURVIVAL GUIDE

In 2024, a two-person startup called Anthropic created Claude, an AI system that could perform legal research, financial analysis, and strategic planning at a level that would have required teams of specialists only months earlier. The company reached a $18+ billion valuation with fewer than 500 employees. Meanwhile, IBM—the company that had defined enterprise computing for decades—employed over 280,000 people to generate roughly the same market value.

This isn't just a story about efficiency. It's a preview of the organizational physics that will determine who survives the convergence and who becomes a casualty of maintaining yesterday's complexity.

Companies asking "should we adopt AI?" are asking the wrong question. The right question is "how fast can we transform before our competitors do?" This isn't a technology adoption cycle where early adopters get marginal advantages. This is am extinction event where the first companies to achieve convergence will operate with such fundamental advantages that traditional competitors won't be able to respond. Dinosaur analogies become almost impossible to avoid.

A converged organization can identify market opportunities in real-time while you're scheduling your quarterly planning meeting. They can adjust strategies in hours while you're waiting for departmental reports. They can serve customers with personalized precision while you're still segmenting markets based on last year's data. These aren't incremental advantages—they're different orders of magnitude.

(It's important to be vigilant right now against your own resistance machine; in your head, among your colleagues, in the media. AI has hallucinations, AI is unpredictable, AI isn't capable of making these kinds of decisions. All true! But we're at the very *infancy* of this technology and the convergence is already happening, and it's important to know the difference between practical caution and having your head in the sand.)

So the question isn't whether to pursue convergence, but how to navigate the transition without destroying your organization or your sanity in the process. Because here's the thing nobody wants to admit: most companies that attempt this transformation will fail. They'll fail not because the technology doesn't work, but because they'll try to pour new wine into old wineskins—implementing AI while maintaining the organizational structures that AI makes obsolete.

Let's gaze into the crystal ball for a moment, then we can explore how to survive it.

The market will split into three categories. First, the AI-native companies—startups and aggressive transformers who build convergent organizations from scratch or remake themselves completely. They'll operate with 10-20% of traditional headcount while delivering superior outcomes. Second, the walking dead—companies that implement point solutions and talk about "AI transformation" while maintaining their fundamental complexity. They'll spend millions on AI initiatives that deliver marginal improvements while missing the convergence entirely. Third, the resistance fighters—companies that double down on human expertise and regulatory moats, betting they can slow convergence long enough to extract remaining value from their traditional advantages.

Only the first category survives long-term. The walking dead will be acquired or bankrupted within a handful of years. The resistance fighters might last a decade in regulated industries, but they're just negotiating the terms of their eventual surrender.

If you're running a traditional organization right now, you're probably in the walking dead category without realizing it. You've got AI initiatives, maybe even a Chief AI Officer. You're running pilots, implementing chatbots, using AI for customer service. But convergence isn't about adding AI to existing processes—it's about *eliminating the processes themselves.*

Here's your first test: can a new employee access and understand all your organization's information on day one? Not "do they have logins to the systems,"—can they actually find, understand, and use information across all your systems? If the answer is no, you're maintaining artificial complexity that convergence will eliminate. Every barrier between your new employee and total information access is a competitive disadvantage.

The transformation path depends on where you're starting from. If you're a startup or small company (under 50 people), you have the easiest path but the least room for error. Don't implement traditional enterprise systems at all. Skip the CRM, the ERP, the separate marketing automation platform. Build your organization on convergent AI from day one. Use AI to handle information processing, coordination, and analysis. Keep your human talent focused entirely on creativity, relationships, and strategic thinking. Your competitive advantage isn't that you have AI—everyone will have AI. Your advantage is that you don't have legacy complexity to maintain, weighing you down.

If you're a mid-size company (50-500 people), you face the hardest challenge. You have enough complexity to make transformation difficult but not enough resources to maintain parallel systems during transition. Your survival depends on speed and decisiveness. Pick a critical business function—sales, customer service, operations—and achieve complete convergence there first. Don't pilot, transform. Eliminate the databases, the reports, the coordination meetings. Let AI handle all information processing for that function. When it works (and it will), move to the next function. You have maybe 18 months to before AI-native competitors start eating your market—that's roughly how long it takes a focused startup to build an

AI-native alternative to what you do, run a few pilot programs, and complete their first enterprise sales cycles. Once they land those first reference customers and prove they can deliver your service at 10% of the cost, the bleeding becomes irreversible.

If you're a large enterprise (500+ people), you have resources but also massive organizational inertia. You cannot transform incrementally—the Information-Commercial Complex embedded in your organization will resist and redirect every effort. Your only option is to create a separate, parallel organization. Stand up a new division that operates on convergent principles from day one. Give it a real business objective, real customers, real revenue targets. Let it compete with your traditional organization. When it starts winning (and it will), you'll face the hardest decision in corporate history: do you shut down the traditional organization that employs thousands, or do you let it slowly bleed out while the new organization grows?

The timing question haunts every executive I talk to. When do you start? The answer is painfully simple: immediately, but not how you think. Don't start with technology selection. Don't start with vendor evaluations. Don't start with pilots. Start by identifying and eliminating artificial complexity in your organization. Every database that doesn't talk to another database—mark it for elimination. Every report that reformats information from another report—kill it. Every meeting that exists to share information between departments—cancel it. This isn't digital transformation; it's organizational demolition. You're clearing the ground for what comes next.

The resistance will be immediate and fierce. Your IT department will explain why systems can't be eliminated. Your compliance team will insist on maintaining current processes. Your middle managers will defend their information fiefdoms. Heaven knows, your vendors will mount a legendary campaign. This is where most transformations fail—not on technology implementation but on organizational will. The resistance isn't irrational. These people correctly understand that convergence threatens their roles. But protecting them means sacrificing your organization's future.

Here's the fortune cookie for CEOs: create a convergence team with exactly three mandates. First, eliminate all artificial information boundaries. Second, reduce coordination overhead by 90%. Third, achieve these goals within 12 months. Give this team absolute authority to eliminate systems, cancel contracts, and reorganize departments. Make it clear that resistance to convergence is resignation in slow motion.

But—and this is crucial—you also need to be honest about what you're protecting. Not every human capability should be eliminated. Creativity, empathy, ethical judgment, relationship building—these remain fundamentally human. The goal isn't to eliminate humans but to rescue humans doing machine work. Your sales team should be building relationships, not updating CRM systems. Your analysts should be developing strategies, not creating reports. Your managers should be developing people, not coordinating information flows.

The successful organizations will develop what I call "convergence consciousness"—the ability to see their organization as an information processing system, like Coase and Williamson did, rather than a collection of departments. Every structure, every process, every role either enables information flow or impedes it. Once you see your organization this way, the transformation path becomes obvious: eliminate impediments, amplify enablers.

Watch for these warning signs that you're doing it wrong: You're maintaining separate databases "just in case." You're keeping parallel processes after transition. You're creating new coordinating roles to manage AI implementation. You're adding AI to existing workflows rather than eliminating workflows. You're measuring success by efficiency gains rather than capability transformations. Any of these signals means you're on the path to joining the walking dead.

The companies that survive will share three characteristics. First, they'll achieve true information convergence—all organizational information accessible to AI systems without barriers. Second, they'll reorganize around human creativity rather than information processing. Third, they'll move fast enough to compete with AI-native startups while being thoughtful enough to preserve valuable human capabilities.

The window for transformation is smaller than most executives realize. The AI-native companies are already here. They're in your market, talking to your customers, offering better products at lower prices with superior service. Every month you delay convergence, they get stronger while you get relatively weaker. The compound effect is devastating—what looks like a small disadvantage today becomes an insurmountable gap within two years.

Some of you reading this will transform your organizations successfully. You'll look back in a few years amazed at the artificial complexity you once maintained. Your organizations will be smaller, faster, more human, and more profitable than you imagined possible.

Most of you will fail. Not because you lack vision or resources, but because the organizational antibodies will prove stronger than your will to change. You'll implement half-measures that increase complexity rather than eliminate it. You'll protect the very structures that are killing you. You'll move too slowly, held back by consensus-building and stakeholder management while your competitors race ahead.

The choice is stark but simple: embrace convergence completely or become irrelevant gradually. There is no middle ground. The filing cabinet created the modern corporation by making information manageable at scale. Databases enabled global enterprises by making information shareable across distances. AI convergence will create something new—organizations that are simultaneously smaller and more capable, faster and more thoughtful, more efficient and more human.

The survival guide is really just three rules: Eliminate all artificial information boundaries. Reorganize around human creativity rather than information processing. Move faster than your competitors.

Everything else is implementation details. The organizations that survive won't be the ones with the best AI strategy or the biggest AI budget. They'll be the ones with the courage to abandon everything that worked in the database era and build something entirely new without talking about “AI” at all.

The convergence isn't coming. It's here. The only question is whether to ride the wave or be crushed by it.

Chapter Ten

POSTSCRIPT: THE MEMORY WE'LL KEEP

I've just spent nine chapters telling you that everything about how we organize work is about to change, that millions of jobs will disappear, and that most companies trying to navigate this transition will fail. Time for a confession of the obvious: I could be wrong about all of it.

Not wrong about the technology—AI convergence is real and accelerating. Not wrong about the economics—the transaction costs that created the modern corporation are genuinely collapsing. But I could be spectacularly wrong about what happens next. Every technological "prophet" is eventually humbled by reality's refusal to follow their script.

The safest prediction in the history of technology is that we'll use it in ways nobody predicted. When Alexander Graham Bell invented the telephone, he thought it would be used to broadcast concerts. When Thomas Edison invented the phonograph, he was certain it would be used primarily for recording dying people's last words. When the internet arrived, experts predicted it would be the world's greatest library. Nobody said "it'll be used to share cat videos and argue with strangers about politics."

So while I'm confident that AI convergence will eliminate artificial information boundaries, I'm much less certain about what humans will do with that capability. History suggests we'll find ways to make things complicated again, because that's what humans do. We solve problems and create new ones. We eliminate inefficiencies and invent fresh absurdities. We build tools to save time and then spend that time doing things that would mystify our ancestors.

Here's something else that should temper my dire predictions: historically, technology that eliminates jobs has tended to create more jobs than it destroys. The catch is that the new jobs are almost always *unimaginable* before they exist.

The filing cabinet eliminated the need for human memory clerks but created millions of office jobs. The database eliminated filing clerks but created an entire IT industry. ATMs were supposed to eliminate bank tellers, but the number of tellers actually increased because ATMs made it economical to open more branches. The internet was supposed to eliminate retail workers, but e-commerce created millions of warehouse, delivery, and logistics jobs that didn't exist before.

There's a pattern here that economists call the "complementarity effect." When technology makes something cheaper, we tend to use more of it, which increases demand for the human roles that complement the technology. When spreadsheets made financial analysis cheaper, companies didn't fire all their analysts—they started doing vastly more analysis, which required more analysts to interpret and act on the results.

Will AI convergence follow this pattern? Maybe. If AI makes it essentially free to start and run a business, we might see an explosion of entrepreneurship that creates more opportunities than traditional employment ever could. If AI handles all routine information processing, humans might discover entirely new categories of valuable work that we can't currently imagine because we're too busy managing databases and creating reports.

I can imagine a future where everyone is essentially a creative director of their own AI-augmented enterprise. Where the question isn't "what's your job?" but "what problems are you solving?" Where the filing cabinet's great-great-grandchildren look back and marvel that humans once spent their days being biological bridges between incompatible databases.

But I can also imagine darker futures. Ones where the complementarity effect breaks down because AI is too good at too many things. Where the new opportunities require capabilities that most displaced workers don't have and can't readily acquire. Where the transition happens so fast that social structures collapse before new ones can form.

The honest answer is that I don't know, nobody knows. We're running an experiment that's never been run before, removing constraints on human organization that have existed since we started externalizing our memory onto clay tablets. We're about to find out what happens when the cost of coordinating human effort drops to effectively zero.

What I am certain about is this: the current system—the Information-Commercial Complex, the artificial complexity, the human middleware between incompatible systems—can't persist. It's too expensive, too slow, and too misaligned with human capabilities. Something will replace it. Whether that something is better or worse for (our present view of) human flourishing depends entirely on the choices we make in the next few years.

The filing cabinet wasn't good or bad; it was a tool that we used to build the modern corporation, which gave us both labor unions and robber barons, both rising living standards and soul-crushing bureaucracy. Databases weren't good or bad, they enabled both global prosperity and surveillance capitalism, life-saving medical research and the Information-Commercial Complex.

AI convergence isn't good or bad. It's a capability—the ability to eliminate artificial boundaries in how we organize information and coordinate human effort. What we do with that capability will depend on whether we approach it with wisdom or greed, imagination or fear, collective purpose or individual gain.

The status quo is ending. The age of the filing cabinet, the database, and the Information-Commercial

Complex is drawing to a close. We're returning to something more fluid, more organic, more aligned with how humans naturally think and collaborate. We're ending the era where organizations had to be shaped by the limitations of their information technology.

What comes next might be the most human era of economic organization we've ever seen—or the least. It might liberate human creativity or make it irrelevant. It might create abundance or deepen inequality. The technology doesn't determine the outcome. We do.

My crystal ball gets fuzzy at this point. All I can see clearly is that the memory we keep outside our heads is about to become as fluid and accessible as the memory we keep inside them. The boundaries between human and artificial intelligence, between individual and organizational knowledge, between thinking and doing—they're all about to blur in ways that would have seemed like magic to the Mesopotamian scribe with his *qan*.

The scribe externalized memory to create civilization. The filing cabinet organized memory to create the corporation. The database digitized memory to create the information economy. AI is about to make memory intelligent. What we create with that intelligent memory will be the story of the next century.

I hope it's a good one.

www.ingramcontent.com/pod-product-compliance
Lightning Source LLC
LaVergne TN
LVHW050921210926
848482LV00012B/489
* 9 7 9 8 2 1 8 7 8 5 5 2 9 *